C000231934

LINCOLNSHIRE
SIGNAL BOXES

Dafydd Whyles

AMBERLEY

First published 2015

Amberley Publishing
The Hill, Stroud
Gloucestershire, GL5 4EP

www.amberley-books.com

Copyright © Dafydd Whyles, 2015

The right of Dafydd Whyles to be identified as the
Author of this work has been asserted in
accordance with the Copyrights, Designs and
Patents Act 1988.

ISBN 978 1 4456 4812 5 (print)
ISBN 978 1 4456 4813 2 (ebook)

All rights reserved. No part of this book may be
reprinted or reproduced or utilised in any form
or by any electronic, mechanical or other means,
now known or hereafter invented, including
photocopying and recording, or in any information
storage or retrieval system, without the permission
in writing from the Publishers.

British Library Cataloguing in Publication Data.
A catalogue record for this book is available from
the British Library.

Typeset in 9.5pt on 12pt Celeste.
Typesetting by Amberley Publishing.
Printed in the UK.

Contents

Introduction   5

1   Newark to Lincoln   6

2   Stamford to Peterborough   11

3   Cleethorpes to New Holland   13

4   Grimsby to Louth, Boston and Werrington Junction   30

5   Brocklesby to Wrawby Junction and Lincoln   35

6   Wrawby Junction to Gainsborough Trent Junction   47

7   Lincoln to Gainsborough   58

8   Nottingham to Grantham   64

9   East Coast Main Line   65

10   Grantham to Boston   67

11   Doncaster to Scunthorpe   77

12   Firsby Junction to Wainfleet and Skegness   82

13   Immingham Docks   87

Acknowledgements   96

Bibliography   96

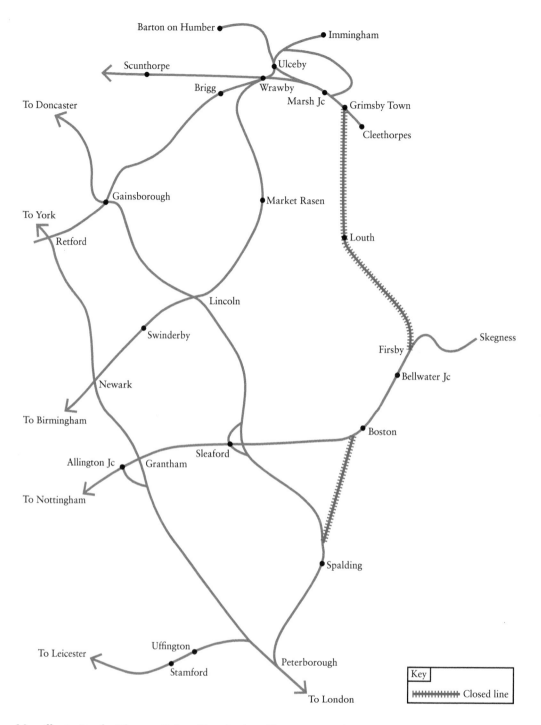

Map illustration by Thomas Bohm, User Design, Illustration and Typesetting.

Introduction

When mentioning the term signal box to most people, they will conjure up an image of the traditional structure with signalmen pulling levers to operate semaphore signals. This is still the reality across many parts of the country, but it won't be for very much longer.

Network Rail have embarked on a programme of 're-control', which will see every signal box in the country close and control moved to one of twelve Rail Operating Centres (ROCs). There, signallers (in the modern parlance) will operate the signalling system from computer workstations. Obviously, all the semaphore signals and wooden level crossing gates will also be swept away in this revolution.

This is purely an interim measure. The next stage is 'traffic management', where computers will run the programmed timetable; signallers will merely oversee the operation and only intervene if something goes wrong or an alteration to the programmed timetable needs to be made.

The next step from there is the removal of all lineside signals entirely, with the signalling system broadcasting 'movement authority' to the computers in train cabs, dictating permissible speeds and the distance ahead clear. The first installation of this is planned for the East Coast Main Line through Lincolnshire in 2018.

A note about the term signalman: I have used it throughout the book, along with signalmen. It is the traditional name for the job, whether done by a man or a woman. I have worked with and been trained by some fantastic signalmen, some of whom also happened to be women. My partner Dorothy is one of the fiercest feminists you could meet, but would hear nothing of the term signaller in her thirteen years in the job.

Chapter 1
Newark to Lincoln

The first railway to arrive in Lincolnshire was the Midland Railway's line from Derby, which was extended from Newark to Lincoln on 4 August 1846.

The British Railways 1960 Sectional Appendix listed manned locations in Lincolnshire at:

Collingham Cottage Lane crossing	Doddington Ballast sidings
Collingham station	Boultham crossing
Swinderby	Lincoln West
Thorpe on the Hill station	Lincoln St Marks

Today the only surviving signal box is at Swinderby, a wonderful Midland Railway type 3a design built in 1901. It retains manually-operated level crossing gates and semaphore signals.

Lincoln St Marks closed along with the station in 1985 when the line was diverted into Lincoln Central station. The site of Lincoln St Marks station is now a shopping centre and the security office there is in the style of a large signal box!

Since 2007 all signalling in Lincoln has been controlled from the new Signalling Control Centre. Eventually this will transfer to the ROC at Derby. Lincoln High Street and East Holmes boxes survive as listed buildings.

Swinderby
The distinctive sight of a Midland Railway signal box at Swinderby. A lovely rural location with crossing gates hand operated by the signalman. Here, the signalman is just reopening the gates after the passage of a train. Although the gates are hand operated, they are still interlocked with the signalling system. Levers in the box release the locks on the gates; once those locks are released, the protecting signals cannot be cleared for a train to proceed.

Looking towards Swinderby box from a footpath crossing at sunset, the signalman can be seen latching the gates open for road traffic to pass. Unusually, here only one gate reaches across the track, the other being set too far back to reach across the line. However, everything is safe as the signals protect the crossing rather than the actual gates. They are there to protect the railway from motorists when a train is signalled. There is no dodging round these gates, as tends to happen at the more modern, automatic crossings.

As a signalman, I can safely say the most important piece of signalling equipment is visible on the right-hand side of this picture! The signalman is locking the crossing gates ready for the next train.

A misty evening develops at Swinderby as the signalman returns to the box after closing the crossing gates to road traffic. Even the station's waiting room windows have been designed with care to their appearance. A truly wonderful location.

Lincoln St Marks

No trace of the original Lincoln St Marks signal box remains, the station now being covered by a shopping centre! However, in a nice touch, an original British Railways-style sign has been incorporated into a replica signal box which serves as the centre's security office.

Lincoln Signalling Centre

The future signal box. Fluorescent lighting and computer workstations. This view of the new signalling centre at Lincoln shows the first two workstations to open. On the left is the city workstation, dealing just with Lincoln station; on the right is the west workstation, which handles trains arriving in Lincoln from the Gainsborough and Swinderby lines. At the time of writing, the signal box has extended further and now controls the line from Lincoln to Peterborough (excluding Sleaford station). Eventually, this box will itself be absorbed into the Derby Rail Operating Centre (ROC).

Lincoln East Holmes

Two former Lincoln signal boxes survive as listed buildings – East Holmes and High Street. East Holmes is a former Great Northern Railway box dating to 1873. It closed in 2008 when Lincoln Signalling Centre opened, but remains *in situ* opposite the university. As with all such structures, it is a great pity that it remains boarded up and out of use. A preserved box that is left to gently rot away isn't much use at all. These structures should be put to community use, or moved to preserved railway sites where they can be fully appreciated.

Lincoln High Street

Left: Also a Great Northern Railway structure, Lincoln's High Street box is brick built and in far better condition than East Holmes. Sited on the city's notorious level crossing, the box looks quite at home among its surroundings. Emergency level crossing control is still possible from the box, so it still has a reason to remain in place. This also mitigates against any community access, which is a pity. Happier days for High Street box as it witnesses steam locomotive *Green Arrow* pass by, working on a charter.

Lincoln High Street

Below: There is another former signalling location on High Street, a few yards down the road from the existing crossing. This is the former crossing box where the line out of Lincoln St Marks box crossed High Street, heading to Market Rasen and Grimsby. The unusual octagonal box has seen a number of uses since closure in 1985, and today serves chips to passing shoppers.

Chapter 2
Stamford to Peterborough

Skirting along the Lincolnshire/Cambridgeshire/Northamptonshire/Rutland border, the second line to arrive in Lincolnshire was also a Midland Railway venture, which was eventually extended to Melton Mowbray and Leicester.

Today the only surviving operational box on the route in Lincolnshire is Uffington, although it sits exactly on the border between Lincolnshire and Peterborough. The former box at Stamford closed in 1984 but was saved by local railway-book dealer Robert Hume and moved a few yards along the line for use as a store room.

Stamford
The Midland Railway's type-2b box at Stamford was purchased by local railway book dealer Robert Hume when the box closed in 1984. It was moved from its position at the west of the station layout to nearer the station and bookshop. At the same time, the station sidings were removed and new car parking provided. Here, Cross Country Trains' TurboStar unit No. 170523 passes the box, working the 1125 Stansted Airport to Birmingham service on 1 February 2015.

A view of Stamford station from the footbridge, with the re-sited signal box tucked in at the far end of the platform.

Uffington

Classified as a Midland Railway type-4a box, Uffington and Barnack was a 1909 replacement for the original box here, provided during the expansion of block signalling with full interlocking. The Midland Railway used prefabricated wooden panels for construction of its signal boxes. They were provided in standard widths of 10 feet, 12 feet, 12-feet 10-inches and 15 feet. The panels were made up at the company's workshops in Derby, transported to site by rail and erected the same day. Strangely, the box only displays the name Uffington, but the track diagram inside shows the correct Uffington and Barnack description. In typical railway style, the box is in neither place, but equidistant from the two!

Chapter 3
Cleethorpes to New Holland

The Manchester, Sheffield & Lincolnshire Railway (MSLR) opened their line from Grimsby to New Holland Pier on 1 March 1848, in conjunction with the East Lincolnshire Railway's Louth–Grimsby line.

The MSLR operated a paddle steamer service to Hull and, in conjunction with the East Lincolnshire's extension to Peterborough, created a fast link between Hull and London.

Grimsby has four level crossings within a quarter of a mile around the station and it was not uncommon to have two closed to road traffic for extended periods as long trains called at the station, or slow moving freights moved to the sidings. Today those problems are rare as no freight trains run through Grimsby station and most passenger trains are formed of only one or two coaches.

Garden Street level crossing is to the east of Grimsby station, where the East Lincolnshire line curves away towards Boston. The imposing Garden Street signal box closed in 1993 but survives today as a listed building.

The line from Grimsby to Cleethorpes wasn't opened until 1863, but the MSLR made up for lost time and invested heavily in developing attractions at Cleethorpes to create a popular seaside resort.

Heading west from Grimsby, Wellowgate Crossing, Friargate Crossing and Littlefield crossings all lost their controlling signal boxes in 1993. Friargate was preserved by the National Railway Museum, but the process of removing the box caused too much damage to a structure that was already in poor condition. Sadly, the remains had to be scrapped as reconstruction was not a viable prospect.

Today, Pasture Street box controls the four-and-a-quarter-mile stretch from Cleethorpes to Marsh Junction, also supervising four level crossings.

New Holland Pier closed in 1981 when the Humber Bridge was opened. Despite fears that this would mean the end for the Barton branch, it survives and has a particularly active user group. The line is a fascinating collection of traditional signal boxes, manually-operated level crossing gates, semaphore signals and even a single line section worked by a train staff. This is all relatively safe as plans to re-control the line from York ROC have yet to be announced.

Pasture Street

Pasture Street box is a BR (Eastern Region) type-19 box, opened in 1964. The window in the rear of the box was for monitoring workings on the line that once ran behind the box to Grimsby Docks. Here, we see the TransPennine Express Class 170 TurboStar unit No. 170306 approaching the box from Cleethorpes with a service for Manchester Airport.

Panel detail in Pasture Street signal box showing the Grimsby station area, once controlled by four signal boxes. The CCTV monitors allow the signalman to see what is happening at level crossings under his or her control. Once the barriers have been lowered at the crossing, the signalman then checks the monitors to make sure there is no one trapped in the crossing before clearing the protecting signals.

The signalman in Pasture Street signal box operating the level crossing control for the barriers outside the box. Note the old-style signal box writing desk, still present in the box from the days when it had a lever frame.

Garden Street

Now manned only by seagulls! The imposing Garden Street signal box at the east end of Grimsby station is a Manchester, Sheffield & Lincolnshire Railway (MSLR) structure dating to 1881. It closed in 1983 when Pasture Street took control of the area, but it survives today as a listed building. Again, sadly, the building is not being put to any use.

Marsh Junction

Marsh Junction box was opened by the Great Central Railway in 1908 in connection with the new dock complex opening at Immingham. The dock was in operation from 1910 but was officially opened by King George V in 1912. When Marsh Junction box was opened, a new east-facing curve was also provided and the box was situated in the middle of the triangle. The east curve diverged to the left in this picture taken from the light railway line from Grimsby Docks.

The west junction at Marsh Junction.

Above: Veteran relief signalman John Bell in Marsh Junction signal box. John started his fifty-year railway career as a telegraph lad in Wrawby Junction signal box and has worked all boxes in his grade between Grimsby and Gainsborough. The Great Central Railway lever frame here dates to the opening of the box in 1908. They are distinctive with their 'jug handle' lever catches.

Right: The signals protecting the main line from the light railway at Marsh Junction – still very much a marsh!

Stallingborough

In 2008, Network Rail provided a new signal box at Stallingborough, replacing the semaphore signals and level crossing gates with coloured light signals and modern level crossing barriers. This view shows why it was necessary to replace the old box! Built in 1884, the Manchester, Sheffield & Lincolnshire Railway box was slowly sinking. Opposite it in this view is the new box waiting to be brought into use.

Old and new at Stallingborough. Still under the control of the old box and semaphore signals, B1 steam locomotive 61264 runs through the station on the rear of a charter train heading to Ulceby to turn. Alongside is the new box waiting to be brought in to use.

Roxton Sidings

Like the old box at Stallingborough, Roxton Sidings box was built in 1884 by the MSLR and is classified as a MSLR type-2 box, noted for its vertical batten boarding and gabled roof. The reference to sidings dates to the opening of the line, when most locations had a small goods shed for local freight traffic such as livestock and general merchandise. Today that has all gone; the box survives purely to supervise the adjacent level crossing and break the section between Stallingborough and Brocklesby.

Roxton Sidings box is set in a lovely rural location and it will be a great shame to see this location changed forever. This was once an everyday sight around the country that is disappearing without anyone really noticing. Then one day they will all be gone and we will be much poorer for it.

The signalman at Roxton Sidings winds the gate mechanism to open the gates after the passage of a train.

The signalman at Roxton Sidings working the block instrument bell tapper to Stallingborough. These three separate wooden instruments are worked together to signal trains between Roxton and Stallingborough. The instrument on the left shows the state of the line going away from Roxton towards Stallingborough, which is operated by the signalman at Stallingborough. The instrument on the right shows the state of the line coming from Stallingborough, operated by the signalman here at Roxton. We can see here the needle is pointing to 'Train on Line'. When the train has passed through the section complete with tail-lamp, the signalman at Roxton will 'Call Attention' to the signalman at Stallingborough, then send two beats followed by one beat, 'Train Out of Section', then use the handle on the instrument to put the needle back to 'Normal', or 'Line Blocked' until the next train is offered.

Ulceby Junction

The line from Grimsby comes in behind the box at Ulceby Junction on the left and was a double track until 1989 when the line was singled. At this time, Ulceby box gained a panel to take over the signalling once controlled by Habrough box, which then closed. The double line leading off to the right is the main route to Brocklesby. This Great Central box was built in 1910 for the opening of Immingham Docks. It once controlled level crossing gates, but these have since been converted to lifting barriers. The box was built at such height to give the signalman better sighting over the new layout.

The line looking towards Goxhill and New Holland, with the route to Immingham curving away to the right. Here, again, the New Holland route connection has been reduced to 'single lead'. These arrangements probably wouldn't be allowed to be made today, as collisions have proved the folly of such money saving ideas. Here, a train for Barton-upon-Humber must travel over the 'facing road' for seven chains (154 yards) in order to serve the platform at Ulceby, which has now been reduced to just one side. However, the real risk is coming off the Barton line, where, if a train were to run past the protecting signal at Danger without authority, there would be a risk of collision with a train on the Up main line coming from Ulceby. In the past these kind of collisions have occurred at similar locations around the country. Here, low speeds and the fitting of the Train Protection and Warning System (TPWS), which activates a trains brakes if it passes a signal at Danger without authority, have made the risk of a collision fall within acceptable parameters.

Bystaple Crossing

Another beautifully rural location. Bystaple crossing and former crossing house. Here the crossing keeper uses 'block repeaters' to indicate whether or not it is safe to open the gates for road traffic. Although the gates here are not interlocked with the signalling system, they are considered to be a part of it. Train drivers are instructed to treat the red circular discs on the gates as 'Stop Signals', and therefore should approach the crossing at caution and not pass over it unless the gates are open to rail traffic and the crossing is clear. Again, these arrangements would not be acceptable in a system being installed today, and in the near future this crossing will be altered to install 'key locks' which interlock the gates with the protecting signals.

Barton Lane Crossing

A variation on a theme at this crossing. Here the crossing gates are interlocked with the signalling, but the signals are what is termed 'Non Block'; they are there purely for protecting the crossing and are operated by the crossing keeper from an outside frame. The former crossing keepers' residence is now no longer in use and, as so often happens, a temporary site cabin has been provided for the crossing keeper.

Here, crossing keeper Dennis Brown operates the outside frame to unlock the gates after the passage of a train, seen heading away towards Goxhill. The gates are manually pushed open and closed by the crossing keeper; no wheel here.

The crossing gates at Barton Lane, with the signals and signal box at Goxhill visible beyond.

Thornton Abbey was an Augustinian abbey dating to 1139 as a priory and 1148 as an abbey. It was closed down by Henry VIII in 1539, but the ruins remain as an attraction run by English Heritage and are open to the public.

Goxhill

Built by the Great Central, the unusual window arrangements at Goxhill box made it unique among other Great Central boxes built at the time. Set in a thriving small village, the box is very much at the heart of the community. These kind of signal boxes are very much missed by local residents when they are replaced by automatic crossings.

As Class 31 No. 31465 disappears towards Ulceby propelling an ultrasonic test train, the signalman begins to wind the crossing gates open for road traffic. Goxhill signal box was opened by the Great Central Railway in 1910, again in connection with the opening of Immingham Docks. A single line connection was provided from the Barton-upon-Humber line into the Immingham complex. The line diverged to the left just behind where the train is in this picture.

Signalman Graham Smith gets to work on the gate wheel at Goxhill signal box.

The block instruments for signalling trains to and from Ulceby. Note that the bell is a different shape from the Oxmarsh bell, thereby giving a different sound and helping the signalman identify which bell has rung – not too difficult in a box with only two bells, but more challenging in larger boxes such as Wrawby Junction.

Block instruments in Goxhill signal box for signalling trains to and from Oxmarsh. The left-hand instrument is used for accepting trains from Oxmarsh. When the handle is moved to the left, it moves the needle to 'Line Clear'. This is repeated in Oxmarsh box and electrically unlocks the last signal at Oxmarsh coming towards Goxhill. On the right-hand side is the corresponding instrument for trains going towards Oxmarsh. When the signalman there accepts a train, the needle is moved to 'Line Clear' and that is indicated on this instrument, telling the signalman that the section signal, known as the 'starter', has been released. Between the two is the combined bell and 'tapper' for sending and receiving the bell signals.

Oxmarsh

Left: Staff collection from the driver of a train returning from Barton-upon-Humber.

Right: Signalman Rick Skye gets to work on the crossing wheel in Oxmarsh Crossing signal box.

Right: Close up of the 'train staff'. The brass plate confirms which section of line the staff applies to. This is important because some locations will control access to more than one single line, so the driver will need to routinely check the staff is the correct one! These simple signalling methods date back to the beginning of signalling and are safe, provided the rules are followed precisely every time. Paradoxically, signal boxes on quiet branch lines such as this are low down the signalling pay grades, but require greater discipline from the signalmen as the built-in safeguards of more advanced systems are not present. As the traveller said to the signalman in Charles Dickens' classic of that name, 'So little to do, but so much depending on it.'

Below: The driver of Class 31 No. 31465 takes the 'train staff' from signalman Rick Skye at Oxmarsh signal box. The line from Oxmarsh to Barton-upon-Humber is single track, so to ensure only one train is on the line at a time a staff is issued to train drivers at Oxmarsh box and surrendered back to the signalman when the train returns from Barton. There is only one train staff for the line and drivers are not permitted to proceed beyond the signal box towards Barton unless they have been issued with the staff by the signalman.

Barrow Road

Another fascinating location on the Barton-upon-Humber branch. Barrow Road box was built by the Railway Signalling Company for the Manchester, Sheffield & Lincolnshire Railway in 1885. At the time, the line extended behind the photographer in this shot on to the pier to New Holland. The remains of these lines can be seen on the left, while to the right, curving away, is the line to Barton-upon-Humber. Today, Barrow Road is relegated to crossing box status and the line on to New Holland Pier has been disused for many years. However, the line to Barton-upon-Humber lives on, despite fears that the Humber Bridge opening would kill the line off. The gates are manually pushed open and closed by the crossing keeper who then clears slots to allow Oxmarsh box's signals to be cleared for the train to proceed.

Lovely evening light at Barrow Road crossing as the crossing keeper closes the gates ready for the passage of a train. The former line on to New Holland Pier continues behind the signal box up the right hand side of the factory.

Above: Home comforts visible in this box, much needed to those exposed to the harsh winds from the Humber estuary. Outside, the crossing keeper can be seen closing the gates ready for the passage of a train.

Right: Close-up of the gate-locking levers in Barrow Road crossing box. The 'hand gates' are sometimes also called 'wicket gates', used by pedestrians. These are locked separately to the main gates as it may be practicable to allow pedestrians to cross for longer than road traffic, depending on the location and circumstances.

Chapter 4
Grimsby to Louth, Boston and Werrington Junction

One of the great 'lost lines' of Lincolnshire, Great Northern Railway's (GNR) Grimsby–Peterborough line connected into the main London line and provided a vital line to the capital from towns and ports of East Lincolnshire.

As seen in the previous chapter, the first section, from Grimsby to Louth, opened on 1 March 1848 in conjunction with the Grimsby–New Holland line. On 3 September of that year the line was extended to Firsby, and on October 1 from Firsby to Boston. The final section to Werrington Junction completed the line on 17 October.

Today, the Firsby to Boston section remains open as part of the route to Skegness, and Spalding to Werrington Junction remains as part of the Peterborough–Sleaford route. In addition, the Lincolnshire Wolds Railway are currently restoring the line around Louth.

Signal boxes along the Peterborough–Spalding route were closed in 2014 with control transferring to the Lincoln Signalling Control Centre. However, boxes at West Street Boston, Sibsey and Bellwater Junction still survive on the Boston–Firsby section.

North Thoresby
Retired Network Rail signalman Ian Short, seen here on volunteer signalman duty in North Thoresby signal box on the Lincolnshire Wolds Railway.

Ludborough

A Great Northern 'somersault' signal protecting the level crossing at Ludborough on the Lincolnshire Wolds Railway. These types of signals were once common throughout Lincolnshire. They were introduced in response to the Abbots Ripton disaster of 1876. Early semaphore signals were slotted in the post, with 'All Clear' being indicated when the arm was inside the post. At Abbots Ripton, south of Peterborough and on the main line to London, a fierce snow storm caused the arms on signals at the signal boxes to the north to become frozen inside the post. As a long coal train was being shunted backwards into a siding, the Up *Flying Scotsman* ran past all the frozen signals which were incorrectly showing 'All Clear' and collided with the coal train. The resulting wreckage was then hit by a north-bound express, resulting in fourteen deaths.

These somersault signals had balanced arms that needed to be pulled to show 'All Clear', and returned to 'Danger' if the wire broke. The idea of slotting the arms inside the post for 'All Clear' was quickly dropped by the Great Northern Railway, although in other areas it continued well into the 1920s.

Sibsey

The Great Northern Railway box at Sibsey was built in 1888 when the Grimsby–Boston line was interlocked. Today the semaphore signals have gone and a small switch panel has been fitted, but the hand-operated crossing gates remain, as seen here with the signalman opening the gates for road traffic after the passage of a train.

Bellwater Junction

Bellwater Junction signal box was built in 1913 by local contractors Harold Arnold & Sons when the new line was opened from Woodhall Junction to provide a more direct line from Lincoln to Skegness. That line closed in 1970 but the box remains, now purely to break the section between Sibsey and Thorpe Culvert. The level crossing here only leads into a field and is rarely used.

Bellwater Junction signal box and hand-operated level crossing gates. Although local contractors built the box, signalling works were carried out by McKenzie & Holland.

Memories of much cosier, happier times for signalmen in the view of the chimney in Bellwater Junction box. Pot-bellied stoves have now disappeared from the health and safety conscious world of modern signal boxes, but they are long lamented by older signalmen.

Bellwater Junction signal box also had a second-hand Saxby & Farmer rocker frame fitted. Here we can see what remains of the original locking, it also now having been converted to standard tappet locking.

St James Deeping

St James Deeping signal box is a lovely brick-built Great Northern structure dating to 1876. The box was closed in 2014 as part of the GNGE Joint Line resignalling, with signalling control moved to Lincoln. A local campaign wanted to preserve the box *in situ*, but Network Rail insisted that it had to be moved. A compromise was reached whereby the box was dismantled in such a fashion as to enable it to be rebuilt somewhere else. At the time of writing the pieces of the box are in storage awaiting a new home.

Chapter 5
Brocklesby to Wrawby Junction and Lincoln

The Manchester, Sheffield & Lincolnshire Railway continued their expansion throughout the county with their route to Lincoln, opening to Market Rasen on 1 November 1848 and Lincoln on 18 December.

The MSLR already had designs on Lincoln and were constructing a line, from Clarborough Junction on their Sheffield–Gainsborough line, to join the Great Northern Railway's line at Sykes Junction near Saxilby to access Lincoln.

In the 1980s, modernisation of the Market Rasen line got under way; the semaphore signals were replaced with colour lights worked from panels and level crossing gates replaced by lifting barriers.

Despite these plans, Wickenby box remains with hand-operated crossing gates, but with a modern panel to work the signals – a real hybrid. One can only assume the scheme ran out of money!

Brocklesby
Another box built when remodelling in connection with the opening of Immingham Docks was carried out. The railway was built across land owned by the Earl of Yarborough, and, in a deal to allow the line to be built, an extravagant station was provided at Brockleby. The signal box is sited on the Down platform opposite the station building. The station closed on 4 October 1993 and today is in private hands. The signal box will survive after it closes as it is a listed building, as are the station buildings.

Here, Class 31 No 31459 powers through with a test train from Grimsby.

A Freightliner Heavy Haul coal train passes through Brocklesby station with a load of imported coal for West Burton power station.

New Barnetby Crossing

The crossing gates at New Barnetby with adjacent footbridge for pedestrians. The gates are normally closed to road traffic and only opened when requested, subject to the permission of the signalman at Barnetby, using No. 59 lever there to release the keylock. There is an alternative, if slightly longer, route to avoid the crossing, so most locals use that. The frequency of trains on this busy stretch of railway means road users can potentially have a long wait for permission to cross.

Barnetby East

Left: Sunrise at Barnetby as a steel train makes its way out of the sidings and heads to Immingham Docks.

Right: A rear view of the Great Central type-5 box at Barnetby East, with local operations manager John Stocks on the signal box steps.

Early morning at Barnetby and heavy fog as a Cleethorpes–Manchester Airport service passes, worked by TransPennine Turbo unit No. 170306. 'Fog and falling snow' is a historic term in railway signalling. Traditionally, special rules applied to the running of trains in these conditions, such as greater distances of clear track ahead of signals before trains were allowed to approach. However, with advances such as TPWS, better train headlights and braking capabilities, these precautions are no longer standard. Indeed, the term 'fog and falling snow' has been replaced in the *Railway Rulebook* by the term 'poor weather'.

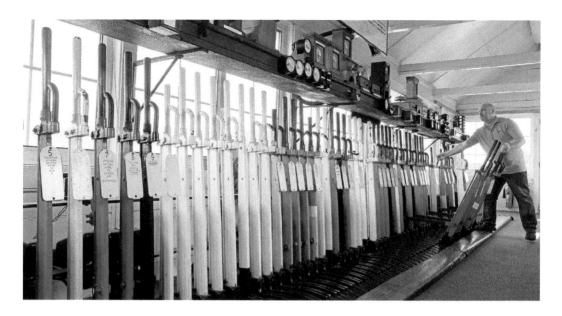

Signalman Tony Powell at work in Barnetby East signal box. Note here the presence of both blue and black levers. Black levers operate mechanical points, and blue levers are the corresponding facing point locks. These are rarely seen these days, the more common arrangement is for both point operation and locking to be carried out electronically and worked by one lever. In these cases, the lever is painted half-black and half-blue. Point levers and facing point lock levers are traditionally the heaviest and hardest to operate.

Signalman Tony Powell in Barnetby East box answers the bell from Wrawby Junction on the Fast Line. The nearest block instruments show that both the Down Fast and Down Slow lines have trains in the section, and the track diagram indicates another train on the Down Fast waiting to follow.

Above: Wooden block instruments in Barnetby East signal box, used for signalling trains on the Down Goods line. Alongside is a now redundant block telephone.

Right: With levers reversed for a train in each direction, the signalman at Barnetby East uses the brief lull before they arrive for a quick drink of tea.

Wrawby Junction

Left: The 'wire run' and rodding leading from Wrawby Junction box. Wires operate mechanical signals where the metal rods are used for mechanical points. The short concrete posts carrying signal wires were once a regular, if often overlooked, part of the traditional railway landscape. Even these are now being replaced by metal posts!

Below: Signalman Nick Jevic in Wrawby Junction box. This magnificent box has a huge 137-lever frame, another Great Central frame with the distinctive jug handles. The box and frame both date to 1916 when changes were made to the layout in connection with the opening of Immingham Docks.

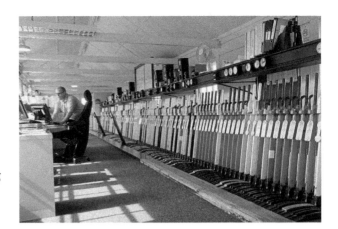

Signalman Nick Jevic consults the train-running computer system TRUST before deciding on his next move.

This block instrument is rather unusual and is called a 'Tyers' black box', named after signalling engineer James Tyers.

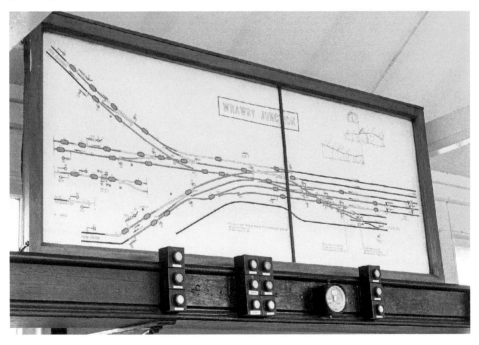

The track diagram inside Wrawby Junction box. Barnetby East is on the right-hand side of the diagram, with lines leading off to Scunthorpe in the top left-hand corner. Below them is the Brigg line leading to Gainsborough, with the Lincoln line branching off to the bottom left.

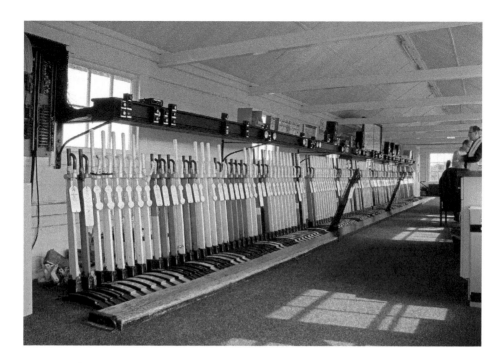

An unusual feature of the 137-lever frame in Wrawby Junction is that some of the levers have letters rather than numbers to identify them. This was done during alterations to the frame and was thought to be easier than renumbering the entire frame. Levers A and B, alongside white levers that were C, D and E, are at the west end of the frame.

Sunset for Wrawby Junction semaphores. Looking west at sunset from Barnetby station to the magnificent array of signals that will soon be sadly lost.

Holton-le-Moor

The signalman in Holton-le-Moor box acknowledges a friendly toot from the driver of a Humber Refinery–Kingsbury tank train. The panel here was fitted in 1989 when British Rail re-signalled the line, with several boxes being absorbed into the area of control of neighbouring boxes.

The signal box at Holton-le-Moor dates to 1890 and was built by the Manchester, Sheffield & Lincolnshire Railway. The neighbouring hut was once used by lamp men for storing paraffin signal lamps.

Wickenby

Beautifully restored, the signal box at Wickenby is another 1890 MSLR structure. Further budget cuts in the 1989 resignalling scheme meant the crossing gates here were retained, rather than being converted to lifting barriers.

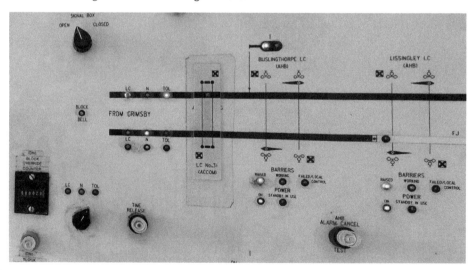

Panel detail from Wickenby signal box. The level crossings at Buslingthorpe and Lissingley once had their own signal boxes to supervise them, with full gates across the road. Today, modern automatic half-barriers are provided, but these type of crossings are prone to misuse by motorists playing Russian roulette with trains, with the inevitable consequences from time to time. Note here how the block instrument is incorporated into the panel; LC indicating 'Line Clear', and TOL for 'Train on Line'. The actual indication is TOL, showing a train is on its way from Holton-le-Moor.

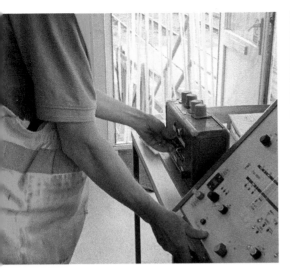

Above left: Signalman Tim Wilkinson returns the key locks to the instrument and answers the block bell from Holton-le-Moor.

Above right: Signalman Tim Wilkinson prepares to close the gates against road traffic.

Langworth

Even older than the signal box, the station building at Langworth was built for the opening of the line on 1 December 1848. Langworth box was built by the MSLR in 1890 when interlocking and block working was introduced to the line. Remarkable survivors that have become part of the landscape, they will be sadly missed when they are gone.

Signalman Greg Sherlock monitoring a level crossing from Langworth signal box.

Signalman Greg Sherlock in Langworth signal box as a trainload of imported coal approaches, hauled by Freightliner Heavy Haul's Class 66 No. 66951. The train is passing the former station, called Langworth-for-Wragby, which closed in 1965. As at most locations, the signal box once controlled sidings on both sides of the line, but today none remain.

Chapter 6
Wrawby Junction to
Gainsborough Trent Junction

The MSLR opened the Wrawby–Brigg section on the same day they opened the Grimsby–Market Rasen line, being just three miles from Wrawby. They were already building the line from Sheffield but had been set back by the collapse of Rother Viaduct at Woodhouse on 30 September that year.

The Brigg to Gainsborough section was opened on 2 April 1849 with the section from Sheffield opening on 18 July, thereby completing a line that ran from Manchester to New Holland, accessing Hull via the paddle steamer.

The Brigg Line survives today as an important freight route, the passenger service having been reduced to a token Saturdays-only 'Parliamentary' in 1989 after attempts to close the line completely were thwarted. Once busy with coal for export, today the flow is the other way, with Russian, Polish and Columbian coal heading to the power stations at West Burton and Cottam.

With the loss of the regular passenger service, the track was rationalised into single line sections. Semaphore signals disappeared except for at Gainsborough Central, but crossing gates worked by wheels still survive at Northorpe, with a hydraulic mechanism working the gates at Brigg. At Bonsall Lane, hand-operated gates survive; at Kirton Lime Sidings a magnificent example of a tall MSLR signal box survives, now listed and recently refurbished.

Brigg
In 1885 the Railway Signalling Company were contracted by the Manchester, Sheffield & Lincolnshire Railway to re-signal their lines in north Lincolnshire, particularly the Gainsborough–New Holland and Wrawby–Scunthorpe lines. Brigg signal box was one of first to be done and is pictured here from the level crossing, with Class 56 No. 56117 passing with a rake of empty coal hoppers for loading at Immingham.

Class 47 No. 47829 was painted into a special police livery for a British Transport Police event. It is seen here running light engine past Brigg signal box.

Signalman Charlie Bailey in Brigg signal box as a Class 66 approaches with a loaded coal train from Immingham Docks. Visible next to the window are the level crossing gates' hydraulic-operating console and mechanical gate-locking device.

Kirton Lime Sidings

Recently refurbished to a very high standard, Kirton Lime Sidings signal box is also a listed building and should survive after the line is re-signalled. It is seen here from the track beneath the road bridge. The sidings diverge to the left and beyond is Kirton Tunnel. In the late 1980s British Rail proposed closing the Brigg–Gainsborough line in order to meet government spending cuts. Thankfully the proposals were defeated, but in an effort to save money the line was converted to single track, with a short double-line section between Brigg and Kirton and an extra passing loop at Northorpe. The passenger service was withdrawn during the week, and subsequently signal box opening hours were reduced, limiting the lines' use for freight.

Kirton Lime Sidings signal box, as seen from the adjacent road bridge, as a loaded coal train from Immingham Docks passes. The sidings for the limeworks diverged left just ahead of the train, but haven't been used for many years and are now secured out of use. The limeworks have left behind a large quarry that has been proposed for household landfill, delivered by rail. Sadly, nothing has yet come of these proposals.

Signalman Bill Rowson in Kirton Lime Sidings signal box as a train heads out of the tunnel and away towards Brigg.

Northorpe
The Railway Signalling Company's 1886 signal box at Northorpe, seen here with Class 60 No. 60010 passing on a Doncaster–Immingham van train. Visible through the box window is the top of the crossing gate wheel.

Northorpe signal box and level crossing gates. The remaining single line has been slewn over to the centre of the formation. The station here closed in July 1955.

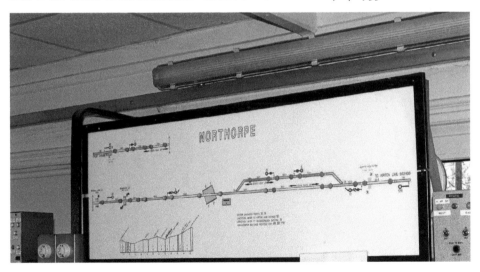

The signal box diagram in Northorpe signal box showing the single line with passing loop. Trains on the single line don't use a token or staff as seen at Oxmarsh, but the line is signalled by the use of acceptance levers. A train is offered on the block bell as normal, then a plunger is pushed which 'sweeps' track circuits between the two boxes to check the line is clear. The signalman at the other end pull the acceptance lever, which then releases the boxes' signal to allow the train to be sent. Once that has been done, the system won't allow another release in either direction until the train has been detected by the system at the other end of the section.

Signalman Simon Doyle in Northorpe signal box, operating the level crossing gate wheel.

Beneath Northorpe signal box, the gate winding mechanism. The pole on the left comes down from the gate wheel in the signal box, this then cranks the rod that pulls and pushes the crossing gates.

'Lever tails' beneath Northorpe signal box. These all used to be attached to weights and pulleys to pull signals and points, but today it is all electronics.

Bonsall Lane Crossing

On the single line between Northorpe and Gainsborough Central is Bonsall Lane crossing. Here, the gate is locked until a road user requires a crossing. The crossing keeper then has to telephone the signalman at Northorpe for permission to open the gates. With no interlocking provided, this is another case where great vigilance and attention is required by both parties.

Gainsborough Central

In the early 2000s, the usefulness of the Brigg line as a freight railway were realised and plans were made to reopen the boxes during the week to cope with increased flows of coal through Immingham Docks. Prior to the scheme getting underway, a managers' inspection train visited the line and is seen here passing through Gainsborough Central station, worked by Class 47 No. 47712. The Manchester, Sheffield & Lincolnshire signal box dates to 1885 and was not part of the Railway Signalling Company's resignalling contract of that year. During the time the line was closed on weekdays, the signal box became a target for vandals and a palisade fence had to be built around it, as seen here.

Seen from the Down platform, Gainsborough Central signal box and semaphore signal.

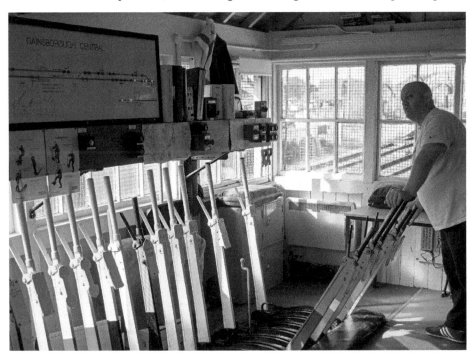

Signalman Eddie Fogarty in Gainsborough Central signal box. The MSLR 'iron brackets' lever frame dates to the opening of the box in 1885. It has since been relocked with tappet interlocking of the levers, but the original type of locking is not known. We do know that the term 'iron brackets' referred to the method of locking, but how it worked is a mystery.

Gainsborough Trent Junction

Frozen points at Gainsborough Trent Junction and the signalman creates a ghostly image in this long exposure picture.

This Gainsborough Trent Junction signal box was built in 1964 by British Rail to replace a structure on the opposite side of the line, a huge Great Central box similar to Wrawby Junction. However, originally there were two overhead boxes at Gainsborough Trent Junction, one at each side of the layout on opposite sides of the river Trent. These were replaced in 1929 when the box on the east side was demolished by a derailed freight train.

The angular outline of the 1964 box at Gainsborough Trent Junction is seen here from the nearby lane. Passing are two new General Electric Class 70 locomotives, Nos. 70020 and 70018 working a diverted Leeds to Southampton container train.

The semaphore gantry at Gainsborough Trent Junction proved rather more difficult to abolish than the engineers imagined. Despite several attempts to uproot it during the work, the gantry stood firm. In the end, to avoid delaying the work, the arms were cut off and the bare gantry remained in place for several more weeks until a much larger crane was brought to site to finish the job! Seen here, the gantry stands defiantly behind the usurper.

The author at the lever frame inside Gainsborough Trent signal box. This lovely wooden-cased track diagram was replaced by a modern board when the semaphore signals were replaced.

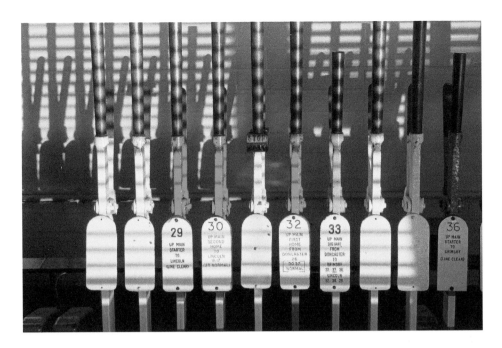

Lever frame patterns on the wall in Gainsborough Trent Junction signal box. Following the resignalling work, Nos. 30 and 32 levers operated colour lights rather than semaphores, and the lever tops were cut short to remind the signalmen not to put all their weight into pulling the levers, as they had needed to do just a few days before! No. 29 lever was also cut short but ceased to operate any signal at all, it being retained purely as part of the mechanical interlocking.

A beautiful sunset's afterglow at Gainsborough Trent Junction, with the semaphore signals and River Trent prominent.

Chapter 7
Lincoln to Gainsborough

This section was opened by the Great Northern Railway on 9 April 1849, a week after completion of the MSLR's Sheffield–Gainsborough line. The Great Northern were building their 'Loop Line' from Peterborough to York via Spalding, Boston and Lincoln as an alternative to their 'Towns' Line' via Grantham and Retford.

Today, the route is controlled from Lincoln Signalling Control Centre as far as Gainsborough, where Gainsborough Trent Junction signal box controls the four-way junction with the lines from Grimsby and Lincoln on the east bank of the River Trent and diverging lines to Doncaster and Retford on the west bank of the river.

At Stow Park, the Great Northern Railways beautiful type-1 signal box survives as a listed building, standing on the Roman road that ran from Ermine Street in the north of Lincoln to Bawtry.

Sykes Lane Crossing
Crossing keepers ready for changing duty at Sykes Lane crossing. The lawn mower has been in use to keep the location tidy. Pride in their work and location came as second nature to most railwaymen (and women!). Class 142021 rattles past with a service for Lincoln.

A lovely location that has now changed forever with the closure of the crossing cabin, Sykes Lane crossing, or in railway parlance No. 318 crossing. The number relates to the number of level crossings on the GNGE Joint Line from Huntington to Doncaster via March, Spalding, Lincoln and Gainsborough. Here, crossing keeper Dorothy Christie closes the gates to road users. The former resident crossing keepers' cottage is on the far side of the line, this too was demolished as part of the 'upgrade' of the line.

Another view of the crossing keepers' cabin at Sykes Lane crossing with gates and resident keepers' cottage. All now gone.

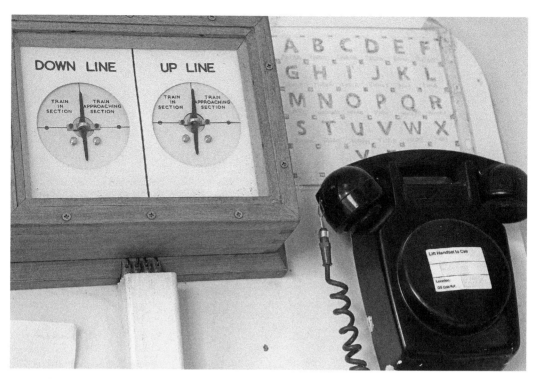

Above: These block instrument repeaters were used by the crossing keeper at Sykes Lane to see if it was safe to open the gates for road traffic to pass.

Stow Park

Left: A closer look at the preserved former signal box at Stow Park, a Great Northern Railway box built in 1877.

Stow Park signal box is a listed building and has thankfully survived the resignalling of the Joint Line, although it is fenced off and not open to the public in any way. Here a diverted Freightliner Heavy Haul load of household waste containers approaches the crossing, hauled by a Freightliner Class 66.

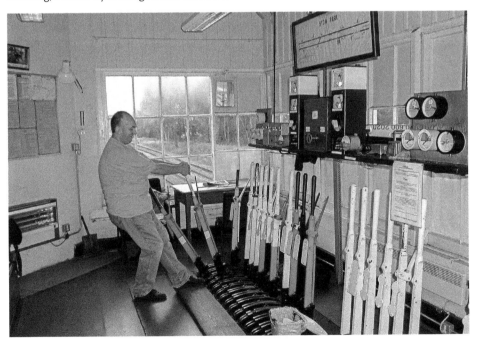

Stow Park signalman Simon Kemp (now sadly deceased) pulls the levers for a train on the Down Line.

Old Lea Station

A rather odd signal box if ever there was one. Old Lea Station box was provided between Gainsborough Trent Junction and Stow Park in response to the Hatfield Colliery spoil tip collapse of February 2013, which blocked the Doncaster–Scunthorpe line for several months. Owing to the very high volume of traffic being diverted via Gainsborough, this box was intended to break the section and increase capacity. However, by the time the box was ready for opening, the tip collapse had been cleared and Old Lea Station signal box was closed and taken away without ever having signalled a train! Here, Class 47 No. 47501 passes the temporary signal box, taking a Greater Anglia coach to Doncaster Works for refurbishment.

Gainsborough Lea Road

Gainsborough Lea Road signal box was a beautiful Great Northern Railway structure, dating to 1895. Sadly, it was badly damaged by an electrical fire in February 2009 and languished boarded up and out of use until 2014, when it was finally demolished.

In happier times, Class 47 No. 47727 passes Gainsborough Lea Road signal box with a Scottish Railway Preservation Society charter from Linlithgow to Lincoln for the Christmas market.

Class 37606 makes a smoky departure from Gainsborough Lea Road at the rear of a track recording test train; sister 37605 was leading.

Chapter 8
Nottingham to Grantham

The first railway to arrive in Grantham was the Great Northern Railway's line from Nottingham on 15 July 1850. The GNR were also in the process of building their 'Towns' line from London to York, and that would open through to Retford two years later on 15 July 1852.

Today, only the box at Allington Junction survives, but this is a new-build standard design that was built for the remodelling of the connection with the Sleaford line in 2005.

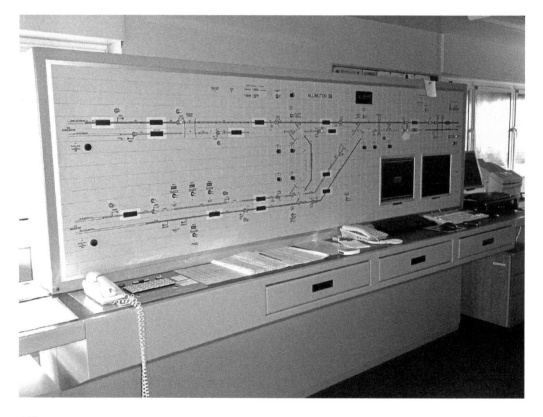

Allington
The signalling panel in Allington Junction signal box showing the layout of the new junction. It was provided in 2005 to allow trains running from Grantham to Skegness to avoid using the East Coast Main Line, thereby freeing up capacity on that important route and avoiding a constant source of delay to cross-country trains. This view shows the line from Skegness and Sleaford coming in at the bottom left corner and curving round to Grantham station in the top left-hand corner. Lines to Nottingham are on the right, and the ability to bypass Grantham station is retained.

Chapter 9
East Coast Main Line

The GNR's 'Towns Line', today's East Coast Mainline, was opened as far as Retford on 15 July 1852. In 1977, modernisation of the signalling concentrated control into new Power Signal Boxes (PSBs) at Peterborough and Doncaster, with the dividing line of control just south of Grantham at Stoke tunnel.

Level crossings were treated slightly differently. All were modernised with lifting barriers and CCTV monitoring, with operation of several crossings concentrated into new crossing boxes.

In Lincolnshire, Tallington, eight miles north of Peterborough, controlled three crossings, including the one outside the box. Further north at Claypole, the existing signal box was retained. A Great Northern type-1 structure dating to 18.. is situated ten miles north of Grantham and controls six level crossings over a three mile stretch of track.

Both these boxes have the ability to be 'switched in' to control trains in an emergency, and the signallers based there are qualified in all the relevant signalling rules and regulations should such a situation be arise. To keep the signallers versed in the operation of the box for signalling purposes, the boxes used to be switched in for an hour on Saturdays, although this is rarely done these days.

Tallington
The modernisation of the East Coast Main Line in the 1970s allowed the introduction of High Speed Trains (HSTs) in 1976, bringing with them a new peak in train speeds of 125 mph. To enable these advances, the signalling of the line was concentrated into several new power signal boxes, such as King's Cross, Peterborough and Doncaster. Level crossings were modernised and control moved to dedicated crossing control boxes, such as this one at Tallington, north of Peterborough. Further modernisation took place on the ECML and now it is fully electrified between London and Edinburgh with trains capable of 140 mph on the line, such as this Class 91 flashing past Tallington.

Claypole

Claypole crossing panel box opened in 1977 and now supervises six level crossings via CCTV. These crossings are within the space of three miles, so will all be lowered at the same time every time a train needs to pass, easing the workload of the signalman and reducing the time the barriers are lowered. When crossings are further apart and signalmen have more crossings to supervise, crossings are inevitably lowered earlier and for longer periods to avoid delays to trains. This is vital in the privatised world of railways, where every minute of delay has to be explained and paid for. Pressures on signalmen in these boxes are very great with the ever-present 'please explain' threat waiting if a train sees adverse signals and suffers delay.

A southbound HST races past Claypole level crossing control box.

Chapter 10
Grantham to Boston

Opened by the Boston, Sleaford & Midland Counties Railway (BSMCR) on 16 June 1857, the Grantham–Sleaford line was operated by the GNR from the start, and extended to Boston on 12 April 1859. In 1865 the BSMCR was absorbed to become part of the GNR.

The route from Grantham was north along the GNR's main line to Barkston Junction, where it branched right. This junction was abolished in 2005 to free up capacity on the main line, and a new curve was built at Allington Junction to join the line that passed beneath the main line heading east.

Today, the line sees an hourly passenger service to and from Skegness and is still controlled by a fine collection of signal boxes with associated crossing gates.

Barkston East

The new box at Allington Junction replaced this 1882 Great Northern Railway structure in 2005. The line leading to the East Coast Main Line and Grantham is seen diverging to the left and was removed when the box closed.

The signal box diagram in Barkston East Junction signal box showing the old arrangements. Below are some wonderful wooden block instruments.

Ancaster
The beautiful Great Northern signal box at Ancaster, built in 1873, is the oldest operational box in Lincolnshire and is seen here with Class 66 No. 66244 passing with a train of empty steel carriers for Boston Docks.

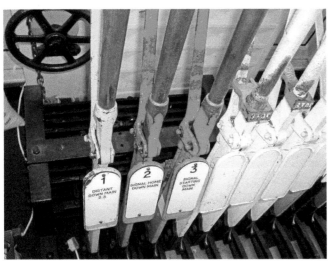

Detail of the lever frame in Ancaster signal box. The wheel on the back wall is for adjusting the tension of signal wires that expand and contract with the temperature outside. In hot weather, the wires tend to get very slack and need adjusting in order for the signal to be pulled off properly. It is not uncommon for the signal to barely move when pulled in hot weather.

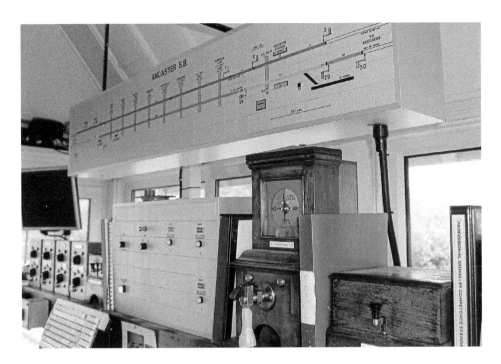

When the new box at Allington Junction opened and Barkston East Junction box was abolished, Ancaster signal box lost its traditional signal box diagram and gained this modern version, seen here above the traditional wooden block instrument that works to Rauceby signal box.

Rauceby
Rauceby is a wonderfully rural Lincolnshire location. Here the signal box on the right is seen opposite the former station building with its unusually tall chimney stack. The signalman is attending to the crossing gates which are still operated by hand.

Sleaford West

Sleaford West is a Great Northern Railway structure dating to 1880, again provided in connection with improved interlocking and block working. It is seen here with a diverted East Coast service passing through at a time when the northbound avoiding line was out of use.

A Central Trains service from Lincoln passing the gates at Sleaford West signal box. Note that the box is reflected in the mirror, which has been erected on a post to help the signalman judge approaching traffic when deciding when to 'swing' the gates; these type of crossings not being fitted with flashing road lights.

The signalman in Sleaford West signal box keeps his eye on road traffic ready for winding the gates.

Lever detail in Sleaford West signal box. The 'lever lead' tells the signalman what the lever does. This plate shows there are three routes available from this signal on the local line; to the Shunt Spur, to the Up Main and to Sleaford North. It also shows what other levers must be operated before this lever can be moved.

Sleaford East

Above: The 1882 Sleaford East signal box can just be seen beneath the wonderful station footbridge as pedestrians begin to cross the level crossing after the passage of an East Midlands Trains HST service to Skegness.

Left: These two levers in Sleaford East signal box that controlled the two approaching single lines from the east, from Heckington on the Skegness line and Sleaford South on the Joint Line. Both have since been removed when a panel was fitted in Sleaford East in 2010.

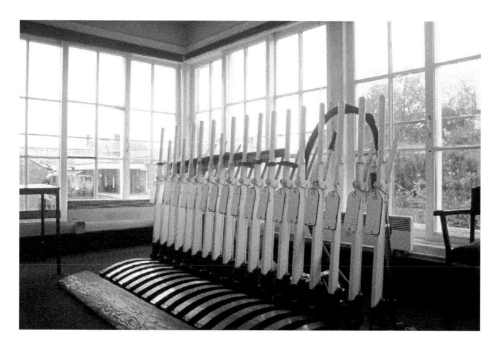

The lever frame in Sleaford East signal box was made redundant in 2010 when a new panel was fitted for operation of the signals. However, as Sleaford East is a listed building, a section of the lever frame was retained.

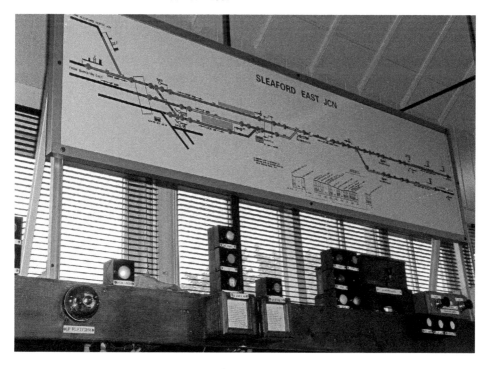

The old signal box diagram in Sleaford East signal box before the panel was fitted. On the right-hand side the two single line routes can be seen, the lower one to Sleaford South and Spalding, the one above to Heckington and Skegness.

Heckington

Left: A beautiful Great Northern box dating to 1876, and in a wonderful setting next to the village's five-sail windmill, Heckington box is still blessed with semaphore signals and a manually operated crossing gate, although the semaphores have now been mounted on new steel posts.

Below: Heckington box is as much a part of the scenery in the village as the windmill and surrounding buildings. Modern flashing road lights here would be sacrilege.

Right: The lever frame in Heckington signal box is a second-hand 1925 Saxby & Farmer rocker. This has since been relocked with standard tappet interlocking, but the old rocker mechanisms have been left *in situ* on the lever frame. These rockers were designed to keep the locking in place while the lever was moving, a great step forward in lever frame design when these frames were introduced in 1871, with an improved version being introduced from 1874.

Hubberts Bridge
Below: British Rail built the box at Hubberts Bridge in 1966 because the existing one was collapsing into the adjacent South Forty-Foot Drain.

West Street Boston

A Great Northern Railway box dating to 1874, Boston's West Street signal box is seen here from the station adjacent to the busy level crossing, complete with its protecting semaphore signals.

Boston Docks

The other signal box in Boston is this unusual octagonal structure that can be found on the branch into the docks. It is manned by docks staff when the daily steel train runs, and has traditional somersault-style signals to protect the crossing. The famous Boston 'stump' can be seen here beyond the crossing.

Chapter 11
Doncaster to Scunthorpe

What is the main route to the east coast at Grimsby and Cleethorpes today was one of the last in the county to be opened. A single line railway, built by the South Yorkshire Railway and River Dun Navigation Company, opened from Doncaster to Thorne along the banks of the canal on 11 December 1855. Passenger services began the following year with a paddle steamer service along the canal to Keadby, where connections were made with traffic on the River Trent. The canal link was no longer needed from 10 September 1859, when the railway line was extended into Lincolnshire to reach Keadby.

Six years later the discovery of ironstone at Frodingham on the east bank of the River Trent gave impetus to take the railway across the river.

By 1967 there were eleven signal boxes in the Frodingham area to deal with the huge volume of traffic associated with the steelworks. Today, the massive steel complex, at what is most commonly known as Scunthorpe steelworks, is still a major source of rail traffic in the area. However, all signalling is now concentrated into Scunthorpe power box which opened in 1973.

The area is not without signalling interest however, as an 1886 Railway Signalling Company signal box remains at Medge Hall, now downgraded to crossing box status with control of the signalling done by Doncaster PSB. Just over a mile further east is Godnow Bridge crossing box, a brick cabin built in 1999.

Keadby Canal Junction signal box also remains, solely for the operation of the sliding bridge that carries the railway over the Stainforth and Keadby canal. Keadby also marks the boundary of signalling control between Doncaster and Scunthorpe.

Further east, the boxes at Appleby and Elsham remain, but are scheduled to close in December 2015 with control passing to the York ROC. Both boxes are listed buildings and should survive beyond their closure dates.

Medge Hall
Situated alongside the Stainforth and Keadby Canal, Medge Hall now just supervises the adjacent level crossing, the signalling being under the control of Doncaster PSB. The signal box is an 1886 box built by the Railway Signalling Company for the Manchester, Sheffield & Lincolnshire Railway. Here, the crossing box is undergoing refurbishment as Class 56 No. 56078 passes with a container train from Immingham Docks to Doncaster.

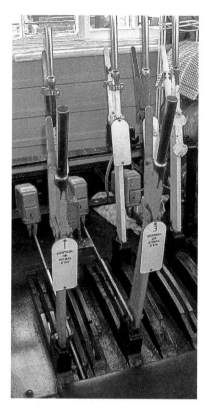

Left: These levers in Medge Hall box control the protecting signals for the crossing. The signals are worked by the signalman at Doncaster PSB, but they will only clear for a train to proceed when these slotting levers are cleared. A key is locked into the frame by these levers. When the levers are reversed and the signals show Proceed, it is impossible to remove the key from the frame to unlock the gates. When both levers are placed in the frame, the key can be removed. Annunciators sound in Medge Hall signal box to give the crossing keeper good warning of an approaching train, allowing them to decide whether or not there is time to allow a road user to cross.

Godnow Bridge

Below: The crossing box at Godnow Bridge is a 1998 structure, built by Railtrack to replace the original Railway Signalling Company box that was in a very poor state of repair. As with Medge Hall, Godnow Bridge has lost control of signalling and now just supervises the adjacent level crossing. Here, the crossing keeper comes out to open the gates for road traffic.

Right: A mirror is often found at signal boxes with crossing gates to help the signalman judge the position of road traffic when preparing to close the crossing gates. Here, the crossing box at Godnow Bridge is reflected in the mirror as a steam locomotive is hauled past.

Keadby Canal
Below: LNER signal box and LNER steam locomotive. Built in nearby Doncaster by the LNER in 1937, A4 No. 60009 *Union of South Africa* passes Keadby Canal Junction's signal box with a charter from Cleethorpes. Keadby Canal box no longer has control of signalling, other than for protection of the sliding bridge and an adjacent level crossing. The box was built by the London & North Eastern Railway (LNER) in 1926. Signalling here is controlled by Scunthorpe PSB, with Keadby Bridge crossing keepers controlling the slots.

With the bridge slid out of position, river traffic is now able to pass. The rail ends lead into the canal, making for an alarming sight, but the bridge is fully interlocked with the signalling system to prevent trains approaching when the bridge is open or unlocked.

Scunthorpe
The signalling panel in Scunthorpe Power Signal Box (PSB). Signalman Dick Swain sorts paperwork for a special out-of-gauge load that needs to be dealt with while Margaret Spencer discusses a track circuit failure with Signalling Manager Andy Reynolds.

Appleby

Above: In 2003, the semaphore signals and wheel-operated crossing gates at Appleby and Elsham were removed and control moved to a panel in an adjacent temporary cabin. The 1885 Railway Signalling Company signal box was then refurbished to a very high standard ready to receive the new panel. The box is seen here on its reopening in 2004 and looks absolutely superb.

Elsham

Right: Given the same treatment as Appleby, Elsham signal box is seen here looking magnificent as Freightliner Heavy Hauls Class 66 No. 66530 passes with a set of empty coal hoppers for Immingham Docks.

Chapter 12
Firsby Junction to Wainfleet and Skegness

Hard to believe today, but Skegness was once marketed as a quiet seaside village where bathers could enjoy peace and quiet, free from bustle at reasonable expense. The opening of the GNR's East Lincolnshire line brought visitors to Burgh, where omnibus transfer was available to Skegness.

The traders and residents of Wainfleet and Skegness saw the difference the railway had made to nearby towns such as Louth, Burgh Alford and Boston. Pressure started to build for a link to the railway, which eventually bore fruit on 11 September 1871 with the opening to passengers of the Firsby to Wainfleet line, extended to Skegness on 28 July 1873.

The residents of Skegness, numbering little more than a thousand on the opening of the railway, could not have imagined what effect the vast numbers arriving would have. In 1880, 50,000 people arrived in August. Two years later the figures were even higher. To cope with ever increasing traffic, the line was doubled in 1900. Word spread, and in 1927 one Billy Butlin came to see what all the fuss was about. His famous holiday camp opened in 1936 and the rest, as they say, is history.

The GN type-1 box at Skegness dates to 1882, but was extended to cope with a new frame on doubling of the line. The Wainfleet box also survives, built on doubling. The wooden crossing gates have now gone but the semaphore signals remain. Further west at Thorpe Culvert is a 2003 modern brick-built box that replaced the previous GNR structure that was slowly collapsing.

Thorpe Culvert
The Great Northern Railway box at Thorpe Culvert, dating to 1881, was slowly collapsing and had to be replaced. A temporary box was provided to house a signalling panel to allow the old box to be demolished and a new one built. Known by the regular signalmen here as 'the fish tank', it was perched above the relay room to allow them good sighting over the adjacent level crossing.

While the new box was being built on the site of the old one, a temporary structure was supplied to house the signalling panel.

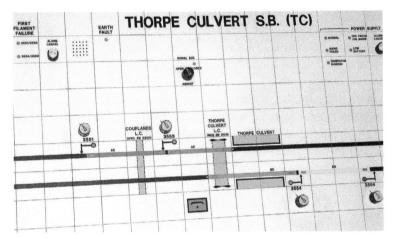

Detail of the panel in Thorpe Culvert signal box.

Wainfleet
Another location where the signal box blends in nicely with the local surroundings, although the lifting barriers and flashing lights of the level crossing are a retrograde step from the previous wooden gates.

Signalman Tom puts his back into the gate lever to unlock the gates after the passage of a train.

Above left: The signalman's lever cloth rests on the gate lock lever in Wainfleet signal box. The beautiful gate wheel dominates the foreground.

Above right: A look beneath the signal box at Wainfleet reveals this interesting inscription.

Skegness

The 1882 Great Northern Railway box at Skegness. The line from Wainfleet was built as a single line but, such was the growth of traffic, double track was provided from 1900. To accommodate the new lever frame required for the enhanced layout, the signal box had to be extended at the far end.

Lever details in Skegness signal box. Not all mechanically operated points had associated facing point locks. In these circumstances, trains carrying passengers were not allowed over the points unless the points had been clamped in position. Every signal box had a supply of these ready for unexpected movements, or for when the points had failed and needed to be manually cranked into position. Points without facing point locks were usually found on goods-only lines or on parts of the layout not normally used by passenger trains.

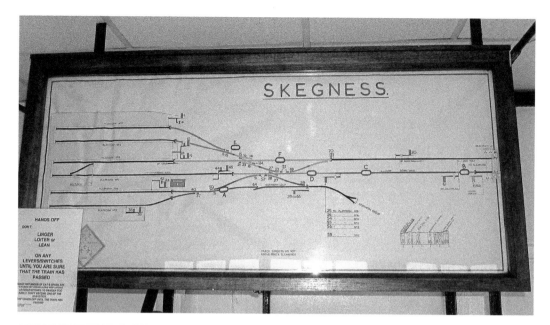

Above: The signal box track diagram in Skegness box. The area in the bottom right-hand corner of the diagram was once a mass of carriage sidings. On summer Saturdays, almost all seven platforms would be constantly filled with arriving locomotive-hauled trains from all over Yorkshire and the Midlands. These would need to shunt to the sidings to free up space or run the loco round to form a quick departure.

Left: The Jolly Fisherman. Forever associated with Skegness, it was actually a creation of artist John Hassell who was employed by the Great Northern Railway to paint publicity pictures for use on railway posters. Famed for the 'Skegness is so bracing' slogan, here is the aforementioned fisherman outside the station with the signal box visible through the doors.

Chapter 13
Immingham Docks

As trade increased through the port of Grimsby, it soon became clear that greater capacity was needed, both on the railway side and on the dock side. Prone to silting and requiring constant dredging, Grimsby was no longer able to cope. Six miles along the coast at Immingham, conditions were far more favourable on the port side; in 1906 work began to provide a new rail terminus.

Three routes were built into the new port. The Grimsby District Light Railway, built as a contractor's railway and used in constructing the port, ran from Marsh Junction, Grimsby, to access the port from the east. The Barton and Immingham Light Railway ran into the port from the north via a connection at Goxhill on the line from New Holland, but the main route into the port was from the west at Ulceby Junction, just as it is today.

The MSLR had become the Great Central Railway in 1897 and was known for its boldness and innovation. In 1901, the British Pneumatic Railway Company had been formed by John Patrick O'Donnell, formerly of Evans O'Donnell. They supplied a low pressure pneumatic signalling frame to the London & South Western Railway (LSWR) at Grately between Salisbury and Basingstoke.

Subsequently, these type of frames were supplied to several locations on the LSWR, and were also improved to incorporate automatic operation of signals.

The next stage was to trial electrical operation of the frames, rather than air pressure, and these were the frames installed in the new boxes on Immingham Docks and are still in use today.

Immingham West Looking rather battered despite its bomb-blast protection, Immingham West box is a 1912-built Great Central box, provided for the opening of the new dock complex.

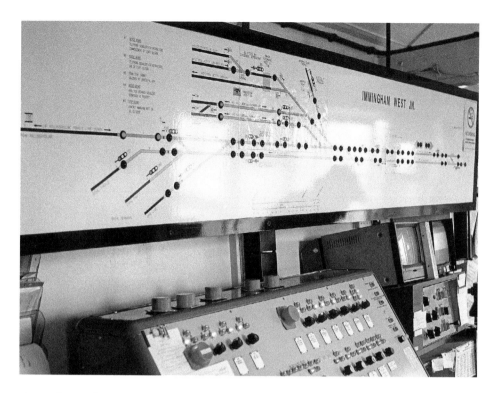

A switch panel was fitted in Immingham West signal box in 1975. Here, the signal box track diagram is seen above the panel and level crossing controls.

Immingham Reception

Semaphore signals still survive at Immingham Reception, as seen here. A GB Railfreight coal train can be seen preparing to depart from coal sidings beyond the box. Immingham Reception box opened in 1912 and was also fitted with bomb-blast protection, particularly important given the strategic location.

Top: Detail of the slides at Immingham reception signal box.

Above left: Signalman Tony Bradley at work on the Lindsey Refinery panel in Immingham reception signal box. The push-and-pull slides for operating signals and points can be seen running along frame behind the signalman.

Right: The power for the signalling equipment is monitored in this fearsome looking device that looks like it belongs in a science-fiction film.

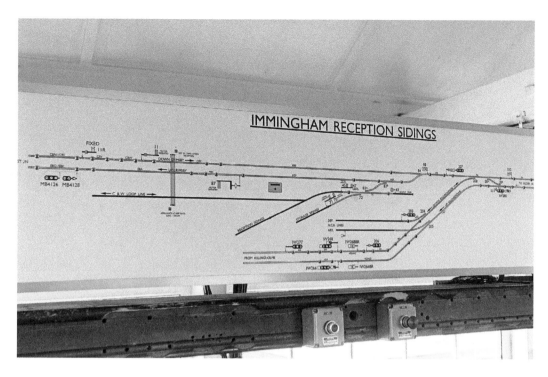

Detail of the signal box track diagram in Immingham Reception signal box.

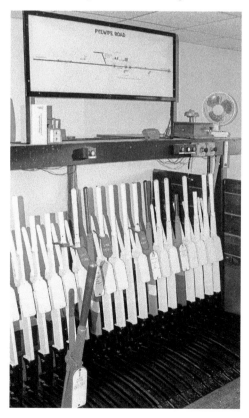

Pyewipe Road

Above: Local operations manager John Raper in Pyewipe Road signal box.

Left: Lever frame and signal box diagram in Pyewipe Road signal box.

Right: The gate wheel at Pyewipe Road signal box is now disconnected, the gates being pushed across by hand. Here, token pouches hang from the gate wheel. These pouches make it easier to transfer the token between signalman and train driver.

Below: Class 31 No. 31459 approaches Pyewipe Road signal box working a track inspection special. Notice that the driver is holding the token out of the cab window ready to hand to the signalman.

Great Coates No.1

Above: Class 66 No. 66061 passing Great Coates box with a diverted coal train from Immingham Docks to Cottam power station. The once extensive sidings are no longer in use, evidenced by the much-rusted rails. Immingham and District trams once rumbled over the bridge.

Left: The mind really does boggle at the sight of this beer bottle, wedged into the roof of Great Coates No. 1 signal box! Class 60 No. 60044 approaches with a loaded iron ore train for Scunthorpe steelworks.

Block instrument in Great Coates No. 1 signal box for signalling trains to and from Marsh Junction signal box.

Immingham East

The original box at Immingham East before it was demolished and a new structure was provided on Network Rail land rather than on docks property. The impetus for this was the lack of spares for the electrically operated signalling slides which needed attention. It also allows Network Rail to move the signalling into the York ROC, something not yet planned for the other signal box on docks land.

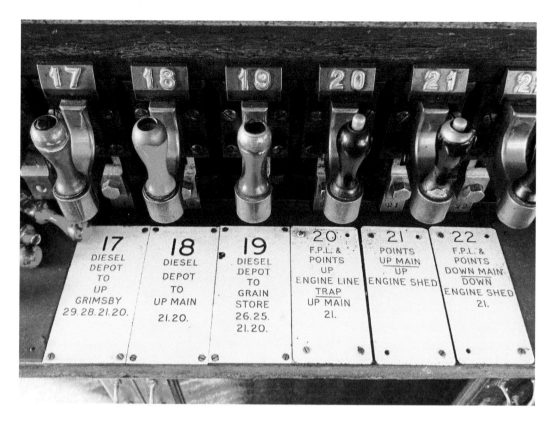

The slides of the old power frame in Immingham East.

The new signal box at Immingham East, quite stylish as modern structures go.